House Training Guide for Your Golder Retriever

Everything You Need To Know For

Effective House Training

Table Of Contents

Introduction

I want to thank you for choosing this book, 'House Training Guide for Your Golden Retriever - Everything You Need To Know For Effective House Training.'

Did you just bring home a golden retriever puppy? Does your excitement know no bounds? Are you excited to start training them and teach them basic commands? Well, you have come to the right place!

Anyone who owns a golden retriever will tell you they are the best breeds in the world. Not only are they intelligent, but also take command quite easily. They are also extremely family-oriented and will go to great lengths just to keep their family happy.

You need to offer them the same open-hearted love and affection that they shower you with, but these simple-minded creatures can be quite a handful if not trained well. So, it is your responsibility to ensure that your puppy is trained from a young age so that they can grow into a responsible and well-trained adult.

In this book, we will look at how you can go about training your puppy and teaching them the basics, including potty training and walking on a leash. You will know when it is the right time to get them started with the training so that it sticks for life.

By the time you are done reading this book, you will be raring to put the advice to practice and to start training your precious pooch! Once your retriever is trained with the basics, you will see that they are nothing but a pleasure to have around.

Let us begin!

Chapter One: Reading your Golden Retriever

Before you go about training your golden retriever puppy, it will help to understand their body language.

When you wish to understand your golden retriever puppy, you have to look at their body as a whole, but it can also help to read their individual body parts. Reading their body language will help you understand them or what they are trying to communicate. Once you get used to it, you will realize that dogs are quite communicative if you just pay attention.

Here are things to look out for:

Reading facial expressions

Their eyes, ears, mouth and tail will all have a tale to tell. Just like how humans use expressions to emote feelings, animals, too, use their ears, mouths and tails to signal emotions. With just little practice, you will be able to assess what your pet is thinking.

Here are some of their feelings explained:

Eyes

If your puppy's eyes are relaxed and oval-shaped, then it signals that they are calm and happy. If they are wide and rounded, then it means they are alert and might also be frightened. If your puppy is staring straight at you, then it means they are threatening you. Dogs avoid making eye contact, but if they do, then it means they are feeling like confronting you.

If your dog looks away from you, or looks at you once and looks away quickly, then it means they do not wish to be aggressive. They are trying to be submissive and are not threatened by you.

If your puppy is showing a whale eye, which means it is round and wide open and staring at you from the corner of the eye, then it means they are about to get aggressive or are thinking of becoming aggressive. It is best to move away from them in such a case.

Ears

Golden retrievers have large and floppy ears, but they might not be as expressive as some of the other breeds. If their ears are being held flat back, then it shows that they are being negative or nervous. If their ears are high and forward-facing, then it means they are feeling confident; sometimes they raise their ears high if they are startled by a noise or are scared.

Mouth

Dogs showcase emotions using their mouths by keeping them open, closing them, curling them inwards to show their teeth, or licking their lips. If your puppy's mouth is closed or slightly open, then it means they are relaxed and calm. When they start licking your face then, it means they are being friendly and submissive and are not being confident in themselves. Yawning is a gesture that dogs make when they feel stressed or tense; it can help to relieve their tension.

If your dog is showing their teeth, by pulling the upper lip upwards, the bottom lip downwards and starting to growl, then it means they are feeling aggressive and might end up biting.

If your puppy is feeling submissive and wishes to please someone, then they will pull their upper lip upwards and show their teeth, but their body language will be calm. Also, their ears will be pinned back and they will not growl. If they do become aggressive, then they will stand tall and start growling or snarling.

Tail

A common mistake that pet owners make is to assume that a wagging tail signals that the dog is happy. This is not always true as it can also mean the dog is being confident, aggressive or cautious.

If the tail is held up naturally at the body level, it means the puppy is feeling calm and happy. If the tail is held low and in between the legs or is tucked underneath the body, then it can indicate a scared dog. If the tail is held in a natural position that is lower than their body and they are slowly wagging it, then it means they are feeling excited. If the tail is being held up high in the air and it is being wagged from side to side in a slow motion, then it shows the dog is feeling dominant and is being aggressive.

Your Golden Retriever's Feelings Based on Body Language

Now that we have looked at the dog's different body parts, let us now look at the dog's body language as a whole.

The best way to do so is by looking at their posture, facial expressions and how they move their tail around. Sometimes, the same facial expression might indicate different feelings.

As a basic rule, your dog can only do three things using their bodies. These are:

- appear larger and be more threatening
- be smaller and less threatening
- hold a natural pose and remain relaxed and calm

Based on these, the facial expressions that they are holding and the way their tail is moving, you will be able to judge how they are feeling.

Happy

If your puppy is happy, then they will look relaxed and natural and will not try to look big or small. They will balance their body using their weight and stand centered on all fours. Their eyes, mouth and tails will all be in a natural pose and their tails will be wagging at their body level or at a slightly lower level. They will look confident and relaxed.

Excited

If your puppy is excited, then they will look happy but slightly less relaxed and a little more alert. If your puppy is excited, then they can wag their tail such that their entire rear will start to move along with the tail. If your puppy is staring at the same thing for a long time, then it means they are feeling excited looking at the item. If they are too excited, then they may end up barking, using short-pitched barks.

Playful

If your puppy is being playful, then they will do the play bow. This is when your puppy bows down with their front legs stretched out in front of them and their chest will lower and touch the ground, while their bum still being raised. They will likely let out an excited bark, keep their mouth open, eyes wide open and their ears alert and high up.

Apart from this, they might jump around and exude a lot of energy, bark in a high pitch to seek your attention and run around, potentially knock things around them over.

Ready for action

If your puppy is feeling alert, then they will stand up tall on all their legs, staring at the object of their desire and their ears will be up and forward. Their tail will be stationary and held at body level, or slightly higher, and eyes will be normal and wide open. If your dog is alert, then they might look a little tense and have a high concentration level.

Angry

If your puppy is angry, then they will try to look large and scary. They will try to remain stiff and cannot be moved easily. Their ears will be forward and eyes will be intense and concentrating on something. Their bodyweight will be centered on their front legs and might be ready to pounce and attack. Their lips may be snarling and they might show a biting reaction. If you spot these signs, then it means your puppy is being aggressive and you will need to take measures to calm them down.

Scared

If your puppy is scared, then they will try to make themselves look as small as possible and become submissive, in order to avoid looking threatening. They will crouch down and touch the floor, place their head on the ground, narrow their eyes and pin their ears back. One of the biggest signs that your puppy is scared is that their tails will be tucked between their legs. They will have more of their weight on their back legs so that they can be ready to start running, at any moment.

Curious

If your puppy is curious and yet unsure of what lies ahead, then they will balance their weight on their back legs and stutter-walk, back and forth. One of their paws might be held forward but their body will be held backward. They will also do interesting actions, such as tilting their head to one side and listen to things they seem to be able to understand.

Submissive

If they are being submissive, then they will show that they are being obedient and passive and won't show signs of aggression. They will not threaten or attack and will try to look small and lower their body, holding their tail high and wagging it from side to side. They will look away and not stare, but lower their head as if they are scared. With that, their neck will also be low and they will have assumed a submissive stance. Other signs are that they might smack their lips, or lick you or another dog, if they are feeling submissive. They may also roll on their back.

Chapter Two: Golden Retriever Unique Characteristics

Golden retrievers are friendly and family-oriented, as they can be sweet, smart and loving to their families. They will be adept at activities like hunting and guiding, and are amazing companions. This makes them very popular and a preferred choice for pet owners.

If you know any golden retriever pet owners, then they are bound to mention some of the following reasons that make them one of the best breeds in the world:

- Golden retrievers are easy to train and they love to please their owners. They like paying attention to what their owners have to say and are willing to do anything in order to please them.

- If you have a golden retriever, then you will know how playful they can be and can be ready to play at any time of the day. As a result, kids will especially love golden retrievers.

- Golden retrievers can get attached to families quickly and will want to be connected with owners at all times, be it sitting or sleeping close by. They will want to snuggle at all times.

- If you own a golden retriever, then you will know that your puppy is always looking forward to having adventures and going out, such as hiking, hunting, running and training.

- Golden retrievers are extremely cute to look at and some of the cuddliest dogs in the world. They can be fluffy and cuddly and are one of the cutest breeds.

- Golden retriever puppies aren't picky eaters. They will eat whatever you give them and munch on anything they think is tasty.

- Golden retriever puppies are very smart and, therefore, easily trained. You can teach them to do almost anything, they learn basic skills easily and perform new tricks without too much effort.

- Golden retrievers are extremely friendly and entertaining. They love to be with guests and might perform tricks just to entertain them. They also make for great pillows and will be up for a cuddle at any time.

Chapter Three: House Training Golden Retriever Puppies

Here are some training methods to adopt to train your golden retriever puppies:

- crate training

- paper training

- constant supervision

- umbilical cord training

All these are easy methods and can help you train your dog with ease.

Let's look at each in detail.

Crate Training

Crate training is one of the most common ways to train your golden retriever. It works on the principles of basic needs, such as a safe den and keeping it clean. Dogs' ancestors, wolves, would nest their young in dens in order to keep them safe. They would also keep these clean in order to maintain a clean and healthy den for their young.

Your puppy, too, will need the same and will look forward to having a clean and safe place to call its own. Crates will make for a great choice as they can keep them clean and will remain safe.

Crate training makes use of crates that will teach your puppy not to defecate where they plan to sleep and stay, controlling their bladder until they get to the designated place. They will learn not to mess up the place that surrounds them.

The crate can serve as the right place for your puppy to be active and alert and should be supervised at all times. If they end up defecating in the wrong place, even once, then you might have to start from scratch.

Here are some pros and cons of crate training:

Pros of crate training:

- Crate training helps to make use of your puppy's natural instincts to keep their surroundings clean and to not defecate where they sit and sleep. This will make it quite easy for you to train your puppy to keep their surroundings clean.

- Crate training can help you take breaks between training. You do not have to keep your eye on your puppy the whole time they are in the crate, especially if they are asleep.

- Crates come with several benefits, such as keeping the puppy from getting into trouble, if you are not watching them.

- If you train your puppy, then they will not defecate indoors, therefore, keeping your house clean.

Cons of crate training:

- One of the cons associated with crate training is that if your puppy has been abused in the past, then they might feel averse to crates. If they were confined to a crate in the past for long periods of time, then they might not take to training very well.

- If your puppy is used to sleeping in dirty surroundings, then they might lose their natural instinct of keeping their surroundings clean.

- Crate training should not be used if your puppy is unwell and is unable to control their bladder.

- If you use a crate to train your puppy for longer periods of time, then it might start impacting them negatively and they might start to feel isolated. You must ensure that you create a positive atmosphere for your puppy and that they aren't left alone when in the crate and undergoing training.

Who is best suited for crate training?

Crate training is best for those who are pressed for time and have only limited hours to train their puppies. If you happen to work for long hours, remain outside your home and do not have anyone who can supervise your puppy, then crate training is not a good choice. You might have to make sure there is always someone who will supervise your puppy and let them out from time to time.

Paper Training

Paper training refers to training your puppy to use the bathroom on a paper or on puppy pads. This can help to control your puppy and where they urinate. Start by placing your puppy in a confined zone where there is tile flooring, so that it is easy to clean up. You can use puppy playpens if you do not have such confinement.

Puppies prefer to eliminate in places that are soft and, thus, putting paper down will give them the right spot to defecate. Try putting papers and puppy pads all over the hard surface so that your puppy can avoid defecating in their crate and will use the paper, as it is able to cover the entirety of the hard surface.

Once they begin to understand what is happening, you can start to eliminate some of the paper area and guide them to using the ones closer to the bed. Simply leave a soiled paper in an area where you want your puppy to defecate; this will guide them to the designated area.

The main goal is to get your puppy to learn to go to the paper and to defecate. Slowly but surely, your puppy will learn to start going outside, instead of remaining indoors to defecate.

Once your puppy goes to the paper, you can quickly open the door and let your puppy go out. Start taking the indoor papers out so that they can defecate only on the outside paper.

Pros of Paper Training

It is one of the best, and easiest, ways to potty train your puppy. It will help your puppy to defecate at the right spot at all times. This is especially useful if you are unable to let your puppy out of the crate every time they need to 'go.' If you happen to live in a place where potty training your puppy outdoors is not an option, then this makes for a great choice.

Cons of Paper Training

If you plan to get your puppy to defecate outside, then paper training can end up being a lengthy process, as your dog has to be taught to go inside the house first and then you have to re-train them to go outside.

If you opt for this method, then you should be prepared to clean up a very stinky mess and to deal with picking up and discarding dirty and soiled papers.

Your puppy will begin to associate papers with a potty and, thus, you cannot leave any kind of paper or newspaper outside as it will be confusing for your puppy.

Who will benefit from paper training?

Paper training is ideal for those who will not be able to let their puppies out if they are out at work.

Paper training can help your puppy have enough room to play around and also learn to defecate naturally. You do not have to intervene, as they will train by themself once they get the hang of it.

If you happen to live in a condo-style apartment, then it might not be easy to take your puppy outside, so the best thing to do will be to train them indoors using papers.

Constant Supervision Training

This is a training method where you do not take your eyes off your puppy when they are being potty trained. You will have to identify the time when your puppy is ready to go to the toilet, as they will begin to circle or start sniffing around. You will then have to scoop them up and take them to the place where you want them to go to the toilet.

This type of training can take quite a bit of observation and knowing exactly when your puppy needs to go. If you are not vigilant, then you might miss the signals and your puppy will defecate wherever they think is right. Even if they end up only doing it once, you might have to backtrack and start training them from scratch.

Pros of Constant Supervision Training

This type of training will give your puppy more freedom and time to carry out their actions. You will not have to buy any type of training equipment and can simply use papers. It is a good idea if you do not wish to use a crate for your puppy, as it is easy to train them using the paper method. It is also a good training method if your puppy has started to go to the toilet in their crate.

Cons of Constant Supervision Training

It can be a lengthy and exhausting process to keep an eye on your puppy all the time. As soon as your attention is diverted, your pup might find a sneaky little spot to defecate.

This method can be time-consuming and take much longer than crate training. If you end up missing out on your pup's circling or sniffing, then they might end up defecating in the bathroom.

You have to devote a lot of time to your puppy and keep a keen eye on them. This is especially important after they have eaten.

Who should use Constant Supervision Training?

This type of training is suited for those who can spend time with their puppies to train them. It is for those who are keen on keeping an eye on their puppies constantly in order to observe their moves and train them to go to the toilet in the right place.

If you happen to have a vigilant personality, then this method can work well for you. You will be able to read your dog's signals well and can quickly train them.

Umbilical Cord Training

This type of training is a variation of the previous type of training. You will be required to watch your puppy to train them and will need a six-foot-long leash to keep them tied up.

Next, you observe your puppy to check if they want to go outside. The leash gives you the confidence that they cannot sneak away when your attention is diverted.

Pros of Umbilical Cord Training

You will be able to train your puppy to wear the leash, be comfortable with it and also to learn to walk with it. You will be able to establish yourself as the leader of the pack and your puppy will take command from you more easily.

Cons of Umbilical Cord Training

You will have to tie your puppy up and make them listen to you, which can be tough if you have a hyperactive puppy. You have to keep an eye on your puppy at all times to make sure they are supervised. If you wish to finish your work in the meantime, then you will have to take your puppy around with you everywhere.

Who is Best Suited for Umbilical Cord Training?

This is suitable for those who like to supervise their puppies and wish to track their moves; it will give you better control over your puppy's movement. You will be able to have your puppy with you wherever you go. You can use the leash to pull your puppy towards you so that you have better control over them. There will also be the added benefit that they don't go to the toilet in the wrong place.

General Tips for Potty Training

Regardless of the training method you use, a few things are universal. They are as follows:

Remember that your puppy won't be defecating inside the house to get back at you, it just means they are unable to control themself.

You have to train your puppy at the right age. Eight weeks is when puppies cannot control themselves for more than two hours. At 12 weeks, they cannot hold it for more than 3 hours, and at 16 weeks they cannot hold it beyond 4 hours.

It is never an option to punish your puppy, as it will not serve any purpose. In fact, it might have a negative impact on your puppy and they might start to associate potty training with punishment. Do not follow the old methods of rubbing your puppy's nose in the poop just to teach them a lesson; this will not work out well.

Puppies who are being potty trained after a nap, a meal or after a playful session will be easier to train. These are the times when they will be ready to go to the toilet.

Your puppy will give you clear signs when they wish to defecate. They will begin to circle around a particular area, or start to squat or sniff. You have to be ready at such times to pick them up and place them in the area where you want them to go.

Most puppies will go back to the same place where they first soiled; they would have made it their own little toilet. If they have done it in the wrong place, then make sure you make them aware of this. This can be facilitated with the use of deterrents.

Whenever your puppy successfully goes to the right place, you should reward them so that they feel special and knows that they will be rewarded for doing the right thing.

Shout out the word "potty" every time you pick up your pup and place them in the right place to defecate. They will then begin to associate the word with the activity. As they grow older, simply saying the word can help them understand what you are expecting of them.

Chapter Four: General Tips to Train your Golden Retriever

Golden retriever puppies can make for some of the most loyal and friendly additions to your family and will be easy to train if you implement the right steps. It is best to train them right from a young age.

Here are some basic tips that can help you potty train your puppy:

Potty Breaks

Golden retrievers like to be trained and love to please their owners. The best way to train them is by giving them more toilet breaks. If you are working with tiny pups, then it is best to take them to the designated spot every hour or so. You have to be vigilant and take your puppy out often; this can prevent accidents and your puppy will be comfortable throughout the training process.

Consistency

Consistency is key when it comes to training your golden retriever. You have to feed and train them at the same time every day. Take them to the designated area at the same time daily so that it is easier for them to make an association and go there by their own accord every day. Just the smell from the previous day will tell them to go to the toilet in the same spot.

Potty Command

Train your pup to defecate outside by following your command, so that there's no confusion and they do what's expected of them. Use words that are easy for them to understand, such as "potty" or "toilet," which can act as signals for them to go to the toilet. Once they understand your command, reward them so that they know they'll be rewarded whenever they do something right.

Crate Training

Many golden retriever owners prefer to use crates to train their puppies. They are suitable for puppies who weigh between 55 and 75 pounds. If you end up getting too big a crate for a small puppy, then use a piece of cardboard to adjust the size. Once they are able to fill in the space, remove the cardboard so that they can comfortably sleep in the crate. Make sure the crate is kept in a room where your puppy can see everyone.

Make your puppy comfortable in the crate and give them their favorite blanket and toys. Leave behind a treat or two for them to enjoy when they're being trained. Try to associate the act of getting into the crate with a positive command. Say, "crate" or "bed" every time you put your pup in.

Mistakes Can Happen

Give your puppy a break in case they end up making a mistake. Puppies are not robots and will make mistakes. There is no point in yelling at them or giving them a tough time if they make a mistake; golden retrievers are especially sensitive. Clean up any mess quickly and get rid of the smell and the stains. Supervise them for the rest of the day to make sure they don't do it again. If you catch them in the act then make a loud noise or clap to startle them, and take them to the designated area.

Veterinarian Visit

It is quite common for your puppy to make a few mistakes until they completely adjust to the schedule. If you think your puppy has started to go back to their old habits or is unable to control themself owing to diarrhea, then take them to a vet to have them examined. They might have an infection that needs to be treated.

Training Older Retrievers

Although most people adopt young puppies, some might also choose to rescue an older dog. In this case, you need to keep some things in mind. If they came from a good home, they might already be well-trained and save you a lot of trouble. In this case, you're in luck. However, if not, you might find it a little more difficult to train older dogs compared to puppies. Older retrievers are a little more stubborn and harder to teach, but not impossible. The real trouble lies with dogs who were in bad homes; some people who take in dogs don't really know how to treat them and end up abusing the poor animal.

Although retrievers are very friendly by nature, a history of abuse can change their behavior. They are warier and are careful and do not trust easily. You need to exercise even more care and patience with these dogs, since they are extremely sensitive and abuse affects them in a huge way. You need to bear with their behavior for a while, so don't startle them or raise your voice to them; always show them affection and speak softly. The first few weeks or months should be used just to gain their trust. They will be watching you closely and react according to your behavior. Give them a treat whenever you can and praise them every time you see them do something good. They are usually more open to children so let the kids play with them. Talk to them whenever you can and know that they will understand.

Although it will take time, they will start to trust you. You already know how to read their behavior, so you should be able to notice their changes. Their body language will show that they aren't as scared as before and they won't flinch when you touch them. Initially, every time you approach them, move slowly and always in line of sight. This way, they'll know that you are coming towards them. Keep a toy or treat in your hand to appease them. In abusive homes, they become instinctively aggressive and might bite if you come near them too suddenly. Bide your time with them and wait till they start hanging around you willingly. No matter what the age, retrievers are fiercely loyal once they trust you. Establish a sense of belonging in them.

Don't let them get away with bad behavior, but reinforce good behavior instead of focusing on the bad. It is pitiful when humans abuse animals who cannot defend themselves and have done nothing to deserve it. Even if it is a puppy or a grown dog of yours, punishment should never be harsh or physical. If they act hyperactively, just ignore them 'til they calm down. If they bite your shoe, make them sit down and give them a good talking to. If you look unhappy about something, they will usually remember not to do it again. They rarely do anything spiteful unless they are extremely angry.

Another thing to remember with retrievers, or any dog, is that you should avoid leaving them alone for a long time. They are quite dependent on your company and can experience anxiety due to separation. If you live alone and are at work for long hours, take them to a dog sitter or dog care center. Do the same when you cannot take them for a trip, but, as often as you can, be with them as much as possible and show them that they are loved.

Chapter Five: Why Training is Important

Getting a puppy home can be a joyous experience for both the owners and the little addition to the family, but it is important to train your puppy.

Here are some reasons why...

If your puppy is not trained to behave a certain way, then they will have to go through restrictions. They will end up sitting at the table to steal food or try to get things from the kitchen countertop, and so on.

They will have to be locked in when you have guests as they cannot be trusted and might end up jumping up to greet them. They might not be able to go on normal walks and end up dragging and pulling, making the person walking them uncomfortable. They might also end up chasing others on the street.

If the family has to travel, then they might have to board them in a kennel or have a supervisor visit to let them out of the crate while they are out.

Now let's look at how a well-trained dog is different:

- A well-trained dog will stay put in the room as the family has their food, as they have been taught not to sit at the table and ask to be fed.

- They are extremely fun to walk with as they have been taught to do so and will walk on command. They will not tug or pull at the leash and not bother other people and dogs on the street.

- They love being with guests, and will sit calmly and only say hello to them on command. They will not climb up on furniture or on the guests, and will maintain discipline.

As you can see, they can have a better life compared to the dog that is not given any training.

Many pet owners make the mistake of thinking that not all dogs need to be trained, as some will be instinctive learners, but this is not true. Dogs will be skilled at learning some basic things, such as keeping their beds and surroundings clean, but will need guidance for other things, such as walking correctly.

Dogs love to receive rewards and will try out a number of things in order to receive the reward. They might also stop certain behaviors just so that they can be rewarded.

Here are some things puppies will naturally tend to do without any guidance:

- They will sit at the table when you are having food or take from the kitchen counter.

- They will start chasing smaller animals around, since it is a fun activity.

- They might end up chewing up your shoes, remotes and table legs, as they will find it relieving and rewarding.

If you do not control these behaviors and tell them not to engage in them, then you can end up promoting the behavior. You must, therefore, tell them not to engage in it and offer alternate behaviors that can be rewarded.

This means that dogs can learn certain behaviors by themselves but only those that reward them personally. It is, therefore, important to teach them the right things to do.

Here are three aspects of dog training that you should know about:

- Puppy training is all about teaching your puppy to do basic things that they should be doing, that they wouldn't do otherwise.

- It is about teaching your puppy to do things that they are not programmed to do and will have to learn in order to stay with their human families.

- It is about teaching your puppy to listen to you and respond to you based on a few simple and basic commands that can help to control them and they can be safely guided through life to be kept safe.

To say the least, puppy training is something all pet owners should take up so that both they and their pups can live harmoniously, and lead a happy and safe life together that is stress free and comes with a few basic rules.

What Are The Positives of Dog Training?

The list of positives for dog training can be rather long, but here are some of them:

- You can keep your puppy safe if you train them from a young age.

- A well-trained puppy will take commands well and act on them.

- They will not eat things they are not supposed to as they will be taught to only eat healthy things that you feed them.

- They will not run out on the streets and will learn to walk with you.

- You can have more fun walks with your puppy as he will walk calmly and smoothly without dragging you along.

- They will be happy if they are allowed to socialize with other people and animals, and will not chase them around.

- They will thoroughly enjoy themselves if you take them out with you whenever you travel, as they will get to see new and interesting things.

- They will have more freedom and will be able to access more places in the house including the garden and porch, if they are trained to act on command.

- Your relationship with your pooch can be stronger if you train them to act on command. There will be less stress and episodes of disappointment.

- You will be able to spend more time with your puppy while training them and develop a close relationship with them.

- Training your puppy regularly will help provide a good opportunity to develop teamwork and go after a common goal.

- Training makes puppies feel good. They like to please their pack and will think they are positively contributing to the welfare of their pack.

- Training them can also give them a sense of importance.

- They will lead fuller and happier lives and so will you.

As you can see, there are many advantages to training your dog to listen to your command.

Chapter Six: Right Age to Start Training your Puppy

There is common misbelief that people have to wait for at least 6 months before training their puppies, but this is incorrect. This advice is given out by traditional pet owners and can end up being the wrong advice. Puppies can be trained from a young age just so that they can be taught the right things, early on.

This idea mainly stemmed from the fact that military dogs are trained rigorously and taught to be physically active right from a young age, which can end up being too overwhelming for puppies, but you will only be teaching your puppy basic commands that might not be as physically intensive.

You will be using a reward-based system where you reward your puppy for displaying positive behavior, so it might not be a good idea to wait 'til your puppy turns 6 months old; they can be taught the basics much before that.

Some might think that 2 months is still quite early for a puppy to be trained, but it can prove to be the right time as your puppy will be enthusiastic and wish to learn new things. In fact, they will be watching and learning from you from the very minute you get them home.

A young and enthusiastic puppy is bound to learn more things than puppies that are older. You can teach them obedience and to do tricks from a very young age. They will take these commands easily and might surprise you at the rate at which they learn new tricks, so it would be best to start training your puppy from 8 weeks. They will be able to take command better at this young age and absorb what you teach them. They will exploit their natural instincts and develop new skills.

This will also be ideal for those who take their puppies everywhere they go. Others will expect your puppy to behave a certain way, so that it is easier to control them and to prevent them from chasing others from a young age. Remember that your puppy is constantly learning and you have to put in an effort to reinforce their positive behavior. You must also make an effort to prevent the negative ones from occurring; it is always better to prevent bad habits than trying to undo them.

It is a good idea to pick up a training routine from an early age so that both you and your puppy can stick to it for long. Training puppies mean spending quality time with them. This can help to strengthen your bond and allow your relationship to evolve. There are many techniques that can be used to train your puppy, including clicker training and shaping.

There is absolutely no need to become physical with your puppy. They have to be guided gently so that they learn what is right and what is not. Force will not be useful, as only a gentle approach will teach them properly.

If in case you were not able to start training your puppy from a young age, then do not worry, as they can still learn once they turn 6 months old, and might be able to catch up if you follow a set training schedule.

It is also possible to train adult dogs by following the right techniques. Simple commands, such as "sit" and "stay," can be taught by rewarding them with a treat every time they obey the command.

If you plan to make your puppy social, then it is important to teach them social skills, as it can help to train them to behave correctly when around guests.

Here are a few simple rules to follow when training your golden retriever puppy:

- Firstly, you need to find an area where there are less, or no, distractions for your dog. Try to do it inside the house because they get more distracted with any passing insects or sounds when they are outside. In the house, it is easier to find a quiet corner to make them concentrate.

- Try your best not to shout at your puppy or correct them when they are only a few months old. They will be too young to understand anything and might end up feeling overwhelmed and scared, so wait 'til your puppy is a few months old. Stay patient and don't show anger or frustration to your dog when they don't learn fast. Negativity will cause the opposite of what you want. They are very sensitive animals and will just want to stay away from you if you display any negative emotions.

- Keep some of their favorite treats on hand to encourage, or even bribe, initially. Food is the easiest way to get your dogs attention. Also keep their favorite toy with you to teach them some tricks, such as to catch.

- It is ideal to keep the training session short and it shouldn't last for any longer than 2 or 3 minutes per day. This is the attention span of your pup and any more means they might not be able to take command effectively. It will also be a stress-free experience for all.

- It is important not to expect too much from your puppy from a young age. Teach them simple commands that are easy to follow. Do not be angry or upset if your puppy is unable to learn new tricks efficiently. Give it time and let them learn at their own pace. Keep it simple and easy to grasp.

- Stay patient and don't show anger or frustration to your dog when they don't learn fast. Negativity will cause the opposite of what you want. They are very sensitive and will just want to stay away from you if you display any negative emotions.

What Commands Can You Teach A Young Golden Retriever Puppy?

There are many tricks that you can teach your golden retriever puppy. Right from house breaking to crate training to socialization habits, you have to teach them many skills to help them have a happy and fulfilled life. Here are some of the commands to take up:

- sit

- stay

- leave it

- roll over

- turn

- crawl

- retrieve

- give shake hand or high five

These are just some of the basic commands that are a must for any puppy.

Remember, it is never too early or late to teach them basic commands. Training has to be a fun and fulfilling activity and you must ensure to follow a set schedule so that it is easier to train your puppy.

Training Your Dog to Learn Some Basic Commands

Your retriever need to learn basic commands, which will help you teach them manners and keep them in line when they're acting up. It is actually quite simple to teach them when they are young, however, it does take a little bit of time and patience. You cannot expect results in a single day and don't try to train them for more than 10-15 minutes at a time. Retrievers get distracted easily and will get bored if you try to do the same thing for too long.

Teach your Retriever to Sit

Teaching your dog to sit is probably the first command you need to deal with. It is a simple and effective way to assert control over them in some situations. Once they learn it, they will sit as soon as you say the word. There are many situations where the sit command is necessary, for instance, when they get very excited upon meeting people. In this situation, make them sit and let the other person greet them calmly.

They also need to learn to sit while crossing the road with you. The sit command is essential when you take them out without a leash. Making them listen and sit with a single command is essential for training.

There are different ways to teach retrievers to sit. Try any of the following ways and use what works on your dog.

The easiest trick to lure your dog into listening is by using treats. Take a treat in your hand and make them sniff it. This will catch their attention and they'll try to grab it from you. Close your fist over the treat and move your hand towards the floor. Usually, they will follow the movement of your hand and move their head up and down. Keep doing this 'til they sit down. As soon as they do, praise them and give them a treat. Do this a few times and then start using the "sit" command as soon as they sit down. Then give them a treat, soon they will get used to the verbal command. After a few days of practice, don't give them any treats but make sure you praise them.

Another way to teach them to sit is by using the command every time they sit by themself. Pay attention to what they're doing all the time and, every time they sit down, say the word "sit" and give them a treat. Soon, they'll realize that they'll get a treat when they go into that position. Do the same thing every few times when they sit down. They'll soon link the "sit" command with the position and listen to you when you command them.

The third method you can use is physical coercion but without force. You should not hurt them in any way or be too forceful. Just use your hands to make them to get down in that position and say "sit" repeatedly. Treat them and keep doing this 'til they learn to sit when you command. Make sure you don't hurt their backbone at any point, since puppies can get hurt quite easily.

Teach Your Retriever to Stay

Once you teach your puppy to sit, they also need to learn to actually stay in that position when you ask them to; sometimes dogs will sit for a few moments but fidget and get up again. Teaching them to stay is required for certain situations. They have to learn to patiently sit and wait when they have to cross the road or at any other time you ask them to.

You need to keep some things in mind when you are teaching the stay command. Firstly, if your retriever is a puppy, they will get distracted and impatient more quickly. In this case, don't make them stay for too long or they'll get bored and move away. Use shorter stay periods for puppies and longer for adult retrievers. Your puppy can learn to stay longer over time. Also, make sure it is a quiet place that doesn't have too many distractions that will make them want to get up. Use treats initially, but slowly reduce them 'til you don't need treats to make them listen.

The first method is to watch their actions normally. Notice when they sit of their own accord and, when they are about to get up, say "sit" and make them get back into position. Then, say "stay." When they listen, throw them a treat. After a while, say "go" to them. Do this a few times every day. Let them learn to associate the words "stay" and "go" with their related actions.

Now use treats to coax them. Go near your dog and tell them to sit. As soon as they do, give them a treat. Now move away and they will try to follow. Say, "stay" and motion them to sit again. Keep doing this 'til they learn and give them another treat. Now throw a treat away from them and say, "go." They'll obviously chase after the treat. After practicing this exercise a few times, your dog will learn to stay in a sitting position and understand "go" as their leaving cue.

To teach your dog to sit for a longer time, use treats again. Make them sit and give them a treat. Wait a few moments and give them another. After a few seconds, give them another. If they try to move, don't give them any treats. Treat them as long as they keep sitting and praise them as they do. After a while, throw one treat away and cue them to go.

Teach Your Retriever to Leave It

Retrievers love to grab things in their mouths, which can be troublesome when it is your favorite pair of shoes or something that can harm them. This is why you should teach them to "leave it" as soon as you instruct them to do so. This command can actually save their life if they try to eat something that would be fatal. It is also useful when they grab someone else's stuff. Strangers don't appreciate their things in your dog's mouth. Remember, don't get physical or rough with your dog for spoiling your things. You might be mad at them but use milder punishment. They don't do it on purpose and it is just an instinct to grab and chew on things, especially when they are teething. Hitting a dog is animal cruelty and completely uncalled for. Instead, be patient and focus on training them well. Just keep certain things out of their reach if they are really important.

Let your dog play with their favorite toy. Now use a treat and ask them to leave their toy. They'll leave it and reach for the treat. Praise them and give them the treat. Teach them this trick with the same object for a few days and then use something different. They should learn to drop anything when you give the command, "leave it." After a while, stop using treats and be assertive when you say "leave it" to them. Keep repeating 'til they listen. Initially, reward their behavior with treats, but later, they'll need to be able to obey the command without treats.

Another way is to just use treats. Sit in front of them and keep a treat in your hand. Now, make them notice the treat. They'll try to take it, but close your fist and say, "leave it." They'll keep nudging your hand for the treat, so keep saying, "leave it." Wait 'til they stop and look at you, then praise them and give the treat. Repeat this a few times 'til they learn to move away from the treat and know you will give it to them. After a while, keep your hand open and move it back a little if they try to take it. Say, "leave it" to make them stop and then say, "okay" and move it towards them to cue them that it is okay. After a few days of using treats, use other things to teach them the "leave it" command. They should know that they have to leave any object when you ask them to.

Teach Your Retriever to Roll Over

Other than the basic commands that will help to discipline your dog, you should try some tricks as well. Watching your retriever perform silly tricks is extremely enjoyable. It is even more fun to show off how smart they are in front of others. Can you imagine how cute your puppy will look rolling on the ground? When you are teaching them to roll over, make sure you find an area that is soft and clean of any debris that could hurt them.

The first method to try is using treats. You also need to teach them to lie down before they learn this particular trick. If they already know it, then continue teaching, otherwise, first teach them how to lie down on command. Now that they are lying down, make them smell a treat in your hand. While they are watching it, move your hand slowly from their nose towards their shoulder. They should be following your hand with their hand. Now, slowly, you should move your hand across their back. They should try to flip onto their back to get the treat. Keep doing this exercise 'til they learn to flip over. Treat them when they do and praise well. The first few times, just use the treat. Then, start saying, "roll over" when they are just about to flip onto their back. Within a few weeks, at most, they will learn to roll over when you say the command. After 5-6 sessions, stop giving them treats and see how they respond. They have to learn to do it without any reward, other than praise. Always remember to praise your dog in order to reinforce good behavior.

There is also another method you can use: make your dog lie down. Use a treat to encourage them to lie on their side. Just guide them and don't use force to push them. As soon as they're on their side, give them a treat. Then, keeping another treat in your hand, motion them towards the opposite side. Keep practicing this 'til they do it and then treat them again. Keep practicing this 'til they roll over faster. After a while, use only hand signals to make them learn to roll over. Soon, you should be able to stop using treats. Start using the "roll over" command as you practice over a few sessions. Giving a little tummy rub every time they roll over will also be encouraging. You might even find them rolling over to prompt you to give them a little tickle.

Teach Your Retriever to Fetch

Golden retrievers are naturally bred to retrieve, so teaching them to fetch and retrieve should not be too difficult; however, some puppies might be easier to teach than others. Once you teach them to fetch, it is much more fun to play with them.

Get hold of your retriever's favorite toy. Move around with it and wave it in front of them. They will instinctively jump around and try to grab it. Keep doing this for a while and then just toss it down for them. When they grab it, praise them and give them a treat. For the first few times, toss it near them. After a while, toss it further away and get them to chase it. Praise them when they run and grab it. Keeping treats in your hand will usually make them come back to you with the toy. Initially, play in a confined area so that they always come back to you and don't wander off elsewhere. Suppose you play in a hallway, throw the toy at the end and when they go to it, praise them. Now clap your hands and encourage them to come back to you, by using a treat. Another way is to keep another toy in your hand; they might leave the first one to come and grab the second toy. Keep repeating this exercise and start using the word "fetch" every time they chase after their toy. Once they learn to fetch and return, you can start playing with them in the park as well. Fetch is a great way to exercise your dog with fun.

Teach Your Retriever to Shake Hands

Shaking hands is a great trick to teach your retriever to greet people. You can teach them to be patient and sit when people come. When you teach them the "shake" command, they can politely greet anyone who holds out a hand to them. It is a neat little trick that is easy to teach any retriever.

First, make your dog sit down. They need to get in the sitting position before you teach them to shake. Now take a treat in your hand and show it to them. Close your fist over the treat before they take it. Now move it a little higher and watch your dog. If they try to stand up, make them sit down again. Now move the treat hand a little higher again and your dog will probably move their paw to grab it while they're sitting. Praise them when they keep batting at your hand. Hold out your other hand and encourage them to shake their paw. Reward them with the treat when they do the right thing. As you repeat the training, start using the command "shake." When they lift their paw, give them a treat; soon, they'll shake when being asked to, without giving them a treat. Just make sure to praise them every time.

All of these above are some of the basic commands that you should teach your retriever. Retrievers are smart and will learn soon enough with a little patience and persistence. Avoid reinforcing bad behavior and always reward good behavior. Remember not to display anger at them at any point and always be kind. Start training your dog as early as you can. If your retriever is not a puppy, you need to be a little more careful with older dogs who are harder to teach; however, remember that all retrievers are, by nature, extremely friendly and will appreciate affection.

Chapter Seven: Making your Puppy Wear a Leash and Collar

It is essential to teach your puppy to wear a leash and collar from a young age, so that it is easier to walk them.

When is The Right Time?

Your puppy will not be able to walk properly and take command until they are 12 weeks old. If you start training them from any time earlier, they might not be able to take command properly.

Allow them to settle in for a few weeks before giving them leash training. It is advisable to wait until your puppy is completely settled in and comfortable with you before taking them for walks.

Before that, they should be accustomed to walk on a collar and leash so that it is easier to take them on the streets, and that there is no pulling or tugging involved. Be warned, it can take them a few weeks to get accustomed to walking on the leash.

Choosing the Right Collar and Leash

It is important to pick the right type of collar and leash to walk your puppy properly. Many pet owners do not realize how important it is and the impact it can have on the activity. It is essential to use a leash that is comfortable for both.

You might feel like going for the cutest one, but it might not be the right choice. You have to look at utility and comfort rather than looks. Only the right leash can help you walk your puppy comfortably.

Here are some tips to find the right collar and leash:

- Go for a lightweight collar that is not too heavy and can be easily used. Ask for recommendations and read up on testimonials to assess the right belt.

- Go for a regular, flat collar instead of a choke chain or correctional chains.

- Go for collars that have snaps or clips attached to them, as compared to buckles. These are easier to put on and take off your puppy.

- Go for a collar that fits well around your puppy's neck. There should be at least a two-finger space between the collar and your puppy's neck.

- Go for a soft and lightweight leash that has good webbing; preferably a soft one, if your puppy is young. You will have to change it to a sturdier one as and when your puppy grows older.

Getting your Puppy Used to the Collar

It is important to get your puppy used to the collar, as you cannot expect them to start walking as soon as you get it. It takes a little time.

Here is some help to get you started right.

Starting Out

Before putting a collar on your puppy, you have to make sure that they are calm and relaxed. They have to be in a good mood and there should not be too many distractions around them.

You, too, have to be calm and collected and remain positive. It is important to teach your puppy by example. The basic idea is to get your little furry baby used to the collar, which can take anywhere from 5-10 minutes. Once they get accustomed to it, it is easier to put the belt on and will take much less time to do so.

Right Fit

It is important for the collar to fit correctly, and your puppy's neck should not feel tight. Insert 2 fingers between their neck and collar to see if there is enough space. Make sure your puppy feels calm and happy once the collar has been attached. Rotate the collar around clockwise and anti-clockwise to make sure it is a proper fit.

Putting the Collar on for the First Time

Calm your pooch down and make them sit in front of you. Gently fasten the collar around their neck. Be patient and do not make a big deal of it. They should not feel like something new is happening and should take it as a part of their training routine.

This is the best time to assess whether it is easy to get the collar on your puppy or not. They should remain calm and unfazed. Praise them and give them a treat so that they know they have done a good job.

Your puppy might scratch over the collar and try to take it off. This is natural, as they might feel a little uncomfortable, but you have to wait until they finish. Allow them to become comfortable in their own way.

If you end up taking the collar off just because they are getting uncomfortable, then you will enforce the behavior, so make sure you do not take it off, even if they start scratching it and exhibiting discomfort.

Once your puppy stops fidgeting, give them a hug and say, "good puppy" or "yes." You can also give them a reward for being calm.

The first time you put the collar on them, you might have to keep it there for 5 minutes or so but not any more. The next time you put it on, extend the time to 10 minutes, and so on.

Ensure that your puppy is under supervision during all times when the collar is on. This is especially important if you have a naughty puppy as they could injure themself.

As a rule, never take the collar off when your puppy is feeling uncomfortable, as that can lead to more discomfort.

The next step is to get your puppy used to the collar. Keep it on even if you are at home. Put it on them and leave it for short intervals. Increase the time the collar stays on them gradually, and take it off slowly. They have to associate it with a positive action. Rewarding them each time can help them understand they should wear the collar to be rewarded. They have to understand that it is a part of their routine and day-to-day activities and nothing unusual or special.

Undertake command training so that they sit down in front of you before having the collar placed around their neck. This will make it easier for both of you.

Be playful when placing the collar and associate playtime, or going for a walk, with it. These will establish a positive connection and they will be excited to put on the collar.

Some puppies will have natural instincts and not put up a fight when you add the collar. Some might not be as comfortable and end up throwing a tantrum. Remember to remain positive and make the right effort to ensure their comfort and yours. Some might take longer and this is natural perfectly natural. Allow them to take their own time.

Once they get used to wearing the collar, you can start attaching the leash.

Getting Your Puppy Used to the Collar

You have to exercise patience when attaching the collar and leash to your puppy. They have to get accustomed to it naturally; some puppies might wear a collar easily but not a leash. You should be patient with them and give them time to get used to it. Maintain a positive attitude and ensure that they understand what you are doing will have a positive outcome.

Preparing them correctly from a young age will ensure they take command well as they grow up. It is easier for you to teach your puppy to not pull or tug, but remain calm when being put on a leash, and to sit 'til they calm down before taking them out.

Here are some tips to train them to walk on a leash:

- First off, do not hold the leash. Once you attach it, leave it loose. Allow your dog to drag the leash around behind them. It should be attached to the collar.

- Do not hold the end of the leash and allow your dog to move around freely. It is best to start with a lightweight leash that is not too heavy for them.

- Make sure you look at your dog at all times and supervise them. If the leash gets caught somewhere, then you have to be around to free it.

- Give them treats so that they feel special and praise them from time to time, so that you establish a positive attitude.

- Lure your puppy to come to the leash and collar, so that they can establish a positive association between the two.

- Go for a soft leash that is easy to hold and won't snap back if it slips out of your hand.

- Also, don't buy a retractable leash, since they are more prone to accidents.

- Attach the leash on your puppy for at least 15 minutes before taking them out for a walk.

Picking up The Leash

Once you get your puppy used to the leash and collar, it is time to pick it up so that you can take them for a walk. It should be done the right way so that it is easier for them to associate it with walking. Let them drag it around for 5-10 minutes.

It is imperative to let the leash remain slack. If there is pressure on the leash, then your dog will begin to start pulling against it.

Hold the end firmly and follow your puppy around wherever they wish to go. Do this for a few minutes, 5 or 6 times a day for a couple of days and you will be ready to move to the next step.

Lead Your Puppy

Remember to always lead your puppy so that you establish yourself as the leader of the pack. You should be commanding them and telling them where to walk instead of the other way around.

This might seem a little tricky at the beginning but you have to avoid putting pressure on the leash and drag your puppy around wherever you want them to go, thinking that they'll learn. This will only make them aggressive or disinterested.

Start off by first luring them towards you by using a toy or a treat (it is best to use the ones they like the most.) Next, get your puppy to follow you around and praise them so that they feel encouraged to do as you say, giving them a treat or two every now and then.

Do this for about 5-10 minutes, several times a day, so that your puppy will be ready for their first proper walk.

Going for the First Walk

If it is the first time you are taking your puppy for a walk, then it is important to adopt the right steps. Attach the collar and leash and let them drag it around for some time.

It is best to walk them inside the house or take them to the garden. This will be an exciting activity for them and you will be able to control them better. Allow them to sniff around and explore everything at their own pace. Let them stand and sniff anything that they find interesting, instead of tugging at the collar to move them. Give them enough time to do their own thing.

Maintain a loose leash and remain consistent with it. You do not want to end up with a puppy who tugs and pulls the leash.

If your puppy is lagging behind, you can lure them to follow you using soft and delicious treats. Give them the ones they love and hold it in your hand to tempt them. This will help them to keep pace with you.

If your puppy likes to pull ahead of you, then you have to go for a different tactic. If they're pulling, then stop right there and do not move forward until they're completely at ease. This will teach them that pulling and tugging will not take them anywhere and will make them remain stationary.

It is best to teach them this indoors so that you can make them understand better, without too many distractions around. Praise them once they learn and give them a treat.

Common Problems That Might Arise

Excited Dog

If your dog is too excited by the leash or becomes anxious when you are putting it on them, wait until they fully calm down. Do not be too excited yourself, as it will rub off on them. Remain calm and collected before adding the collar.

Sit by them and calm them down. Make sure they're not too distracted by objects and things going on around them. They should not get too worked up at the thought of a collar and leash being put on them.

Bites the Leash

If your puppy is biting or tugging at the leash constantly, like it is a personal toy, then it means they're too excited by it. In such a case, do not shout at them, as they will do more of it. You must, instead, remain still and release any tension from the leash. Praise them and give them a treat as soon as they listen to you and let the leash go.

Start walking them normally and encourage them to keep pace with you.

Chapter Eight: How to Exercise your Retriever

Golden retrievers are quite energetic and get bored easily if they have nothing to do all day. When you are house training them, you need to remember that they need a little exercise every day in order to stay healthy and behave well. If they're bored and have too much energy, they will tend to misbehave and act erratically. In order to avoid such things, you have to ensure some regular exercise. Thankfully, exercise for retrievers can be quite fun. You have many different options to choose from and it will also help you to get some daily exercise with them. Make sure they get at least 30 minutes of exercise every day and, if time permits, do this twice a day.

The easiest way to exercise them is to take them for a walk around the block or preferably the park. If they're not well-trained, make sure you put a leash on them and also check the leash laws of the area. The pace of the walk depends entirely on you.

Another fun way is to play fetch with them. Retrievers love a game of fetch; it is easy to throw a ball or stick, for them to chase and come back to you.

Hiking is another great way to get exercise for you and your dog at the same time. Find a trail that is soft and not too steep. It should be fun but not too difficult for your dog. Also, the ground should be clear of anything that could injure their paws.

Running is another simple but effective exercise. Take them for a morning run with you every day, if possible. Start with a slow jog and, if they're well-trained, let them run alongside you. You need open areas for this and if you want to run along roads then choose a time and area where there won't be vehicles moving around.

Swimming usually comes naturally to retrievers. The first few times, make sure you go in with him and use a float if they're scared. Soon, they'll discover that swimming comes naturally to them and they'll learn to love the water. Swimming is especially delightful for them in summer when the heat becomes too unbearable because of their furry coat. Find a pool or lake that allows dogs and let them enjoy the water. You can also just set up a kid's pool in your backyard and fill it with water for your dog to enjoy.

Agility training is a more complex form of exercise. Many retrievers love agility camps and even take it up for competitions, however, it is not suited to all of them, especially if they're sick. Let your dog try some easy jumps, etc. and let them see if they enjoy this type of exercise.

Flying discs are a fun toy to play fetch with, but you'll need to train them to use them first. Once they get the hang of it, you can use a disc instead of balls and sticks. They actually enjoy chasing after the flying toy and grabbing it in their mouth.

Take your dog to a park whenever you can. They love socializing and playing around in nature. There will usually be other dogs for them to play with and they even love meeting new people. It is a great way for you and your dog to be social.

Retrievers may appear to be the healthiest and happiest breed of dogs on earth but they are very prone to illness. You need to keep their diet in check, exercise them and take them to the vet once in a while. Ensure that they get all their shots and any supplements they need. They are actually prone to obesity and heart disease more than other breeds. When they grow older, they also tend to get arthritis, which can be extremely frustrating for them.

When you take on the responsibility of a retriever, make sure you do everything required to take care of them. They will definitely return the love and loyalty for as long as they live.

Conclusion

Thank you again for downloading this book!

I hope this book was able to help you .

Finally, if you enjoyed this book, then I'd like to ask you for a favor, would you be kind enough to leave a review for this book on Amazon? It'd be greatly appreciated!

Below you'll find some of my other popular books that are popular on Amazon . Simply click on the links below to check them out.

https://www.amazon.com/dp/B07L39KV2D

I thank you again for choosing this book and hope you had a good time reading it.

As you can see, it is quite important to train your golden retriever puppy from the right age. Once they start associating training with something positive, they'll begin to enjoy themself.

The training process is not just to teach them tricks and manners, it is also a great way for you to bond with your little pooch. They will trust you more and you also get to enjoy each other's company and understand each other better.

I hope you and your puppy have fun together and enjoy learning and growing.

References

https://www.totallygoldens.com/read-your-golden-retrievers-body-language/

https://www.akc.org/expert-advice/lifestyle/10-things-only-golden-retriever-owners-understand/

https://www.totallygoldens.com/the-best-way-to-house-train-a-puppy-4-popular-methods/

https://pets.thenest.com/golden-retriever-puppy-potty-training-3523.html

https://www.totallygoldens.com/why-training-your-golden-retriever-is-so-important/

https://www.totallygoldens.com/what-is-the-right-age-to-start-training-a-golden-retriever-puppy/

https://www.totallygoldens.com/getting-your-puppy-used-to-wearing-a-leash-and-collar/

35672273R10038

Made in the USA
Middletown, DE
08 February 2019